A HEAVEN WROUGHT OF IRON

POEMS FROM THE ODYSSEY

A HEAVEN WROUGHT OF IRON

POEMS FROM THE *ODYSSEY*

D. M. SPITZER

Etruscan Press

Etruscan Press
Wilkes University
84 West South Street
Wilkes-Barre, PA 18766
(570) 408-4546

WILKES UNIVERSITY

www.etruscanpress.org

Published 2016 by Etruscan Press
Printed in the United States of America
Cover design by L. Elizabeth Powers
Interior design and typesetting by Susan Leonard
The text of this book is set in Adobe Jenson Pro.

First Edition

16 17 18 19 5 4 3 2 1

Library of Congress Cataloguing-in-Publication Data

Spitzer, D. M., 1975-
  [Poems. Selections]
  A heaven wrought of iron : poems from the Odyssey / D. M. Spitzer. --
First edition.
    pages cm
  ISBN 978-0-9903221-3-9
  1. Homer. Odyssey--Poetry. I. Title.
  PS3619.P586A6 2016
  813'.6--dc23
                          2015028575

Please turn to the back of this book for a list of the sustaining funders of Etruscan Press.

This book is printed on recycled, acid-free paper.

This book is dedicated to my teachers
Daniel Levine, Lynne Spellman,
Stanley Lombardo, & John Younger,
each of whom helped me to hear
the music of the ancients;

to Rick Jackson, whose careful reading
& generous support for this project
brought about several fine improvements;

&

to the memory of Ian Clark Spitzer
(1967-2011), *frater, artifex, amicus.*

A HEAVEN WROUGHT OF IRON

PROOEMIUM

I am an epic poet
and the epic poem is gone.

I am a poet in darkness.

ODYSSEY I

TURNING

What is man but turning
out of himself towards
a beyond of difference,
into the region where risk swarms
in the wreckage and buries
the vast reflectivity of air
down into dust?

Who but a god might sing
this flotsam and jetsam creature,
the turning already into otherness,
the othering itself?

"What I will say is bent and wanders
because it knows its course"
[*Od.* 1.179]

"You are the child of suffering.
Upon your face, in your eyes
beauty lingers
for an instant, then
it takes you with it.

Remember all those beautiful ones
who once stormed and raised the dust
in their lengthening shadows?
They ran with your father
and they have gone beyond the sea.

You are the same."

Now muster the only
human reply,
son of pain,
filled with the clear breath
of divinity:

"I do not know myself."

At the end of speech
a grey shimmer
shakes the air
and is already gone.

Behind you and above
in the thin square of light
and red painted tiles,
the heavy, dark wing-beat
of the goddess
pulses the air
around you
alone

and her figure is a
charcoal cloud-bird
drawn on a cave wall,
a vulture's penetrating
shadow with the sharp eyes
of an owl in the dark.

Beneath the heavy cloak of darkness
let a foot
fall
where you cannot see.

A god has cleared the way.

whole night through
there
veiled and alone
[*Od.* 1.443]

ODYSSEY II

ORIENTATION

On the horizon-palm of Dawn
a rose-light blossoms.
In all his suffering
man still rises;
the light raises him.
Light flowers all around him.
He is clothed in it.
It shimmers on the sharpness of mind,
in the swiftness of feet.
In early light
man is just like a god.
But who could hold the dawn?

Presence destroys you.
Those who remember without forgetting
stand in midday and cast no shadows.
They are the architects of identity.

The god will take your place,
her owl-eyes
that pierce the dark
night become your own.
She is not with you.
She is you.
But you are somewhere else.

Evening wells up in things.
The goddess of sea-grey eyes
meets the twilight with dimness
adding veil to veil,
curtains drawn together over the world
showing the shape of things.

Her eyes were born for night.
And her presence is its own mystery,
an evensong lifting itself into the dusk,
a great dark owl soaring towards heaven.

The sun sinks and all paths turn to shadow.
[Od. 2.388]

The way to dawn passes through the night
[Od. 2.434]

ODYSSEY III

GATEWAY

All things are bronze
under the rushing sun.
Whatever dies, whatever remains,
whatever has been turned and ploughed
out of earth—the world is bronze.
The black bulls on the shore
and their bright blood,
the shore and its sea,
the deep-blue god
who shakes the world,
who shakes
a bronze world,
a ringing bell wakes all that moves.

But the earth keeps secrets
sleeping in her folds
and the bell doesn't ring in the dark.
Bronze is the music of light.
To youth, the earth's dark
is silence.

Seek the elders, they have heard
the earth-music,
the weight of their age
bows and bends them
and all the bronze singing
has taught them how to listen.

"The thought of everlasting gods is not swiftly turned.
It is the turning."
[Od. 3.147]

"The storm-gatherer divides
us from ourselves.
He is the god who splits the air,
writes white fires
across a deepening sky,
stirs brothers against
each other.

That night was a long
fissuring gap; even the mind
divides.

One part remains,
propitiating,
one part scatters
over the shining sea.
A third kept turning
across the wine-dark divide.
He is the man of turning.
He is the man of pain.
He is like a god."

At the end of words
a sea-grey shimmer
shakes the air and
is gone.

Behind you
all the massive
midnight wing-rush
of the sea-eagle

beats rings of sound rippling
through you and the dark
and its great shadow pushes
the stars into cover.

Then

    silence

    reverence

    night

That old man is the story of generations.
See the rose-light blossom
on the early fingers of Dawn—
    it has always done this.
Those glistening stone benches
    his father built
hold some dawn-petals in themselves.
And the old face wears
a crown of dawn-roses,
    like a god,
    or a statue
    of a god.
His face is almost glistening stone.
If you look closely
you might see the face of his father
who has already passed
    into the unseen.
His many sons unfold around him
and the dawn-rose light reaches them all.

Another dawn of flowers burns early
and sings another song of beginning.
Two horses shuffle beneath the harness
and shift a chariot on its single axle:
they are every one built to close distances.

Show them the whip and they open
    like doors into dawn-flowering fields,
    like thunderclaps shuddering echoes
    in a hall of light.

Swiftness streams down their glistening backs
and fans out into wheatflames that crackle in their speed.
They travel east.

The sun sinks and all ways turn to shadow.
[Od. 3.497]

ODYSSEY IV

LAKEDAMONIA, OR
THE VOICE OF GHOSTS

Ghosts dwell in the hollows
of darkness where wedding
songs and feasts fulfill
promises of old. Memory
is wed to the passing moment
and the past lives as what is
new.
      This darkness unifies—
      a swallowing cavern,
      a new-moon midnight,
      Aphrodite's dark gold.

        Even in the dark
        these halls shine.
        This is the shine of night—
        bright torches touch
        only the edges of the dark.
        In the depths
        gold and silver
        are moments of earth
        and the marvel
        lies in the identity
        of difference—
        the firelight outlines,
        the continual erasures.

"So many unspeakable things, wonder grips my gaze.
These wonders belong to silence."
[*Od.* 4.75]

This is the place of forgetting.
This is the center of truth.

"The wonder of it all is that you resemble yourself,
a child of suffering."
[Od. 4.142-143]

The salt spray is air
and the air is sun-fire
and in its narrow mouth
the earth holds them,
the elemental language of divinity.

When awareness grasps you
you grasp back.
Hold it still
even as it becomes
serpentine as
the skin where you hid,
waiting.

The truth is the sea,
its wine-bright surface
gathering the heavens, its
teeming deep beyond
your reach and rolling
under its tide.

The god in the deep
counts the protean waters,
knows the number of the sand
on the ocean's floor.

Hold on.
Remember: forget.
Hide yourself from yourself.
Remember: forget.

Go down to the ship and the sea.

Prepare yourself.

Endless night is coming.
[Od. 4.428-429]

a blackened heart full of rage
and eyes burning like blazing fire
[Od. 4.661-662]

Beware of the harbors.
They are a hidden brightness.
A reversal.
The presence that is your nemesis.

ODYSSEY V

DISINTEGRATION

Gods and men must separate
for Dawn to rise
and cleave the eastern edge
of darkness. So the light
is born into this opening
and it is seen
by mortals and immortals alike
and it is good.

Only the gods sit in place
and among them
the great god, the god of sound
that divides the air,
the god whose thunder precedes the dawn.

All at once, the suffering of man
condenses around the
storm-god's daughter
before the gathering light:

> he who has closed the gap
> weeps for a return to the divided world,
> but divinity's embrace is slow to fall.

"you could stay here,
sharing this place with the goddess,
and she would hide you away
and you would be immortal"
[Od. 5.208-209]

"I choose to die because too much light burns."

Now that the mantle of divinity no longer hangs
        upon your shoulders
you must return to earth; sea alone would crush you.
Cloak yourself in the leaves of trees on the bank,
where benevolent water curves into rock and clay
        whence you came.

Return yourself to earth, ready to hold you,
ready to keep the black embers to burn again.
And the sky will catch the smoke.

ODYSSEY VI

LIMINALITY

A breath of air bears
the sea-grey goddess of eyes
to the threshold. She comes
to a standstill
upon your head
and she is a phantom,
a dream,
a girl.

Her smoky voice rises
in your mind:

"Fabric every color of the murex,
beautiful things,
rumors,
a wedding.
Beauty, beauty, beauty!
Move your feet
in the stream,
splash in its current,
lie on its banks.
Do not be careful.
The gods are always near."

heaven a pedestal
of the gods
not shifting not
settling untouched

by wind or rain or snow
a cloudless
blue sky
opens up and a radiance

such is the delight of the gods who are blessed
for all the days of the world
[*Od.* 6.42-46]

A man is a lion born
from the swollen mountain
womb of earth. He is
his strength. Rain, wind,
the flooded waters
do not detain him
in his hunger: he comes down
into the level fields
burning in his eyes
setting fire to all he sees.
Man, a lion among cattle
or swine, lifted face and
swifter than swift deer
in the grass,
in thought.
And his hunger
pushes him
to devour the light-
filled openings he calls
spaces. He sees emptiness;
he is bodied yearning.

ODYSSEY VII

NOSTALGIA

The veil of divinity still
shelters you, an atmosphere
of your own.

Make yourself invisible to men
who would seek to find your
name, let the air of divinity
hold you, anonymous,
as you pass

until you reach the hearth's
grey ashes and smoldering
embers. There you will find
the ships, like dreams,
or smoke—they will bear you home.

Those speeding ships
as quick as a wing
or a thought.
[Od. 7.36]

For now, learn to follow
in the footsteps of a god, leaving
no trace, belonging to air,
open to the silent wonders
of the world.

then the man walked in the footsteps of a god
[Od. 7.38]

This place—as radiant as the sun or the moon
[Od. 7.84]

See that orchard—
> the pear trees grow heavy
> with pears, the shining apples bow
> under their own fullness,
> figs ripen on the fig trees
> standing in the bright places,
> reveling in the light.

Through every season, some things fall while others grow
and the west wind blows over them all.

Learn the seasons of the year.
Learn the seasons from the green and purple vineyard:

> some darken under the sun,
> some have matured into readiness
> for the festive harvest;
> others, already gathered, are there
> to be stomped and to become
> bright-faced wine swirled with
> the depth of oceans
> and to mellow into old age;
> some are not yet ripe,
> while others darken under the sun.

In the orchard and vineyard,
listen for the water.
Beneath them two springs
still murmur and flow.

> Learn their double course.
> Each thing rises in its turn
> and falls again to earth.

Such are the glorious gifts of the gods.

"through all the past
the gods have shone
in brightness to us"
[*Od.* 7.201]

ODYSSEY VIII

GENESIS

In earliness, a birth.

The eastern sky bleeds colors

and the darkness of all

beginning begins withdrawing

itself, transforming itself

into shadow and shade

and the light falls into the dark

falling from below into

the cool, cool dark of dawn.

Dawn resembles dusk.

Goddess of beginnings, Dawn, reaches

into the beginnings, signals

Night's undoing, her atavistic fingers

making the hand the primeval sign.

The dawn-sign and its brushstrokes of saffron

and fading poppies and overripe pomegranate

like the murex palette, like the inside

of the sea-creatures nightfoundered

upon the pale gold sand, the strand, the shore.

The dawn-sign and its brushstroke blood

stain the east and all.

And so they also rise, paired
silhouettes in the beginning, shades
in the mist-filled morning.

If there was a moon last night
it is forgotten.

The moon's disappearance
in the hour appointed for dawn
blazed a signal in the paling sky,
a painted flare in the receding night.

"No matter how strong
you are nothing
binds you to itself
like the sea"
[Od. 8.138-139]

A first step
nearly breaks you,
a bout located
simultaneously
in and out,
home and away.

> This, they tell you, is an athletic world.

You begin as
a stranger
and guest
in hospitality's
grip.
The bounds are
already marked off,
the mule-drawn,
furrow-length duration
of a life.

As your spine
twists in response
the grip contracts
and you squeeze
into the broad arena
for breath,
for the eristic double-move
of respiration,
a reflexive
hurl into
distances.

Unmatched.

A gasp and hush
swallows
all around as you raise
your face
in the morning
wreathed around you,
the stone colored
orbit trace of your discus curl
into being.

In the middle of a quaking floor
smooth and level for the dance,
a floor as wide as the sea
and rattling beneath gleaming feet
of youth, a vortex of browned knees
high in the midday air and wrists
whirl sun-baked hands to heaven.

In the center stands a poet, a singer
        of songs.

This swirl of youth must spin his mind
with its thunderfalls, for the gods took
his eyes long ago.

In the center of bright murex-dyed ribbons and
flashing gold bracelets and bodies animated by song
stands a poet in darkness.
His first song is over now, the tale of men
whose glory spirals to the Olympian
thrones in smoky rhythms and memory.

Now the singer sings the divine.
The song follows the spiral smoke offering
of mortal deeds and finds its place at the knees
of the gods, who glitter darkly
through the agèd green sea-glass song of beginning.

And the song rises: the poet's god is the god
of fire and metal that gleams and reflects the light.
Only *his* gossamer threads of bronze,
a technology of reflection and concealment,
might trace the twofold, beauty's all-too-quick
flight into violence.

A third song returns the voice
to human affairs, to deceit,
to risk, to art and mimesis,
to the wheat-toned flames
on the crystalline sand
and the whitewashed huts
burning in twilight and
the shoulder-bulge pulls on long oars
of ash and to ash spears and their
glistening sharp bronze tips,
to towering overhangs
in the mountainside
and the mesmerizing images
of the gods crafted of wood,
stone, and metal by human hands.

Now the singing traces a holy
trinity of angled turns
out and back, a crescendo swelling
in the ethereal distances from earth
to sky and down again to earth.

A third song descends and the descent
completes the circuitry of song.
In song, men come pouring out
of horses they themselves have built.
The living world, under the spell of
song, opens its myriad-mouthed face
and men like gods pour out.
The fire-filled night, the great city
and its high bronze gates open
like the horses' eyes, the ancient
city sweeps the work of art into its
twilight-grey plaza and waits to be
illuminated and engulfed.

This is the song of encryption
And the way of things, a penetrating
effluence binding gods and men
in their horses made of song
under the ringing bronze sky
and upon deep-echoing earth.

the gods crafted things this way
when they spun out the threads
of human destruction so that song
might rise for the future
[Od. 8.579-580]

ODYSSEY IX

MYTHOLOGY I

"Blessèd is the singer
blessèd the song
blessèd too are those
straining to hear it.

Let the wine swirl and catch
the lantern light within tin-ringing
bowls for mixing.

Let the silver-rimmed cups of gold
collect the sea-dark wine full of flame
as each man lifts a double-handled
cup high to the singer, the song,
and to the gods who give these gifts.

Indeed I praise the song, even
as it stirs up grief
in the hollow place,
even as it retraces the etchings
of hard wandering on the sea's
undulating back, grooved
deep in my face, my hands, and eyes,
by ghost-pale driftwood
and salt sea-wash and split timbers
that once stood tall as masts.

A low moan resounds in my ears, in my
heart. How should I summon all that I
have seen and all that has shaken me
and all that has left these tattoo-grooves
in my skin and thought? How shall I tell these
sorrows, which the Olympian gods gave me?

Now I shall speak my name, so that long after
my shadow has passed beyond the shores
of this bright place those sounds might
echo in these halls, in memory and light.
Call me———call me the man of suffering.
Heaven rings with this."

"As a young man
the world was
a battlefield—noise
like smoke inhaled,
eyes burning,
rolling over men
as stone towers
or spears or oxen
for the altar.

Everything I saw I ploughed under
and the dust billowed behind my swift feet."

*"on they came, men like leaves and flowers
in spring's dawn-glow"*

[Od. 9.50-51]

"You see, we live in three seasons:

first, dawn, and the horizon-chasm
as far as you can see in a still
dim beginning, and the wave-
sparkle and gulls and cormorants
down-swoop to niello fish-scale shimmers
beneath the magic surface of bronze water—

then at midday you stand and
cast no shadow—
the earth-tremble you make
in your stand waves
and beside your beached
ships' black-sleek balance you
remain, a figure of stone,
adamantine, breathing fury,
and any rushing cavalcade
you withstand—

and last, when the sun shifts toward
the time of shadow pools
gathering over footpaths
and byways for bringing in
the broad oxen and the yokes hang
in the oak stable and their clatter-sway
chimes now and again and the fresh hay and straw
crackles under worn-down hooves and flanks—
at this time you are overpowered—
yet you flee, like a fool, and your fellows-
at-arms flee and the bronze flashing
greaves like cymbals fill with noise
a darkening sky of starry flashpoints above.

For now you may escape death, which is fate,
only because another hour is carved out for you."

"The way home is
overgrown,
verdant foliage brushes
over the back-curve
of desire, the supple
cover around its
spine pulsing
with the urge
to wander no more,
no longer to reach
out in longing
for that nexus
of time present and time
past and time
future. Here is the promise
of satisfaction, thickly leafy
and pungent and full
of barbs slicing
desire, draining it
of the reconnaissance
of nostalgia."

"The god who gathers cloud-darkness rattled our ship with the north wind
and he collapsed earth and sea in nebulae of darkness and night fell out of heaven"

[Od. 9.67-69]

"Oblivion is the greatest risk.
          Those who forget without remembering
          stand in midnight
          and cast no shadows.
          They are the attendants of oblivion."

"In the wild monsters live, deep
in caves, barely visible through the vine-
canopy and poplar thickets and laurel
wreaths and tall foliage oaks. The earth
shelters them and the god of storms
draws out of the black island soil
shimmering wheat and bright oats
and vines close to the ground with
grape-clusters, but rising all of them
towards the heavy, dark rain of god.

Circle-eyed and monstrous who
lived there, he fed
on the brain-spattered grey mess
he made of my crew like some
mountain lion tearing dogs to shreds
and leaving nothing behind.
We were closed in the cave
and the light went out
with the terrible figure
and in the dark I groaned
and trembled and sank
          into thought.

In the wild live monsters, tearing at
the sea, scowling at the sea and the bright
air and the gods in their halls
of bronze. And I blinded whatever sight
does not see as I see, but the gods—
the gods are many and each one sees
for himself. And so I learned, slowly,
of the many eyes scanning the world
and the light-spectrum they span.
Some only see in the dark."

ODYSSEY X

MYTHOLOGY II

"Everything is animated—

      the world falls into place as
      male and female, each one
      striving to join the other,
      their stirring like broad
      winds across the open sea,
      like windswept thoughts
      shimmering on the mind's
      bright surface.

Everything is animated
in the double realm.

      All speaking, all singing,
      the oceanic breaths filling
      you, moving you—all things
      are passing along and between
      the seen and the unseen—it is
            the essence of animation.

Every so often things fall
into harmony and fix themselves
immovably, as the center
of a storm, within the wind-sweep
respiration of the world,
falling with each breath, imperceptibly,
into the blanks between, the empty.

"The winds gusting
over the sea's
wide back keep
me in flux.
All my days turn
on the unlooked-for action
of the other,
the lunar pull
from all directions,
and
the quotidian
revolt in me."

"my soul always working
on this one thing

whether to plunge
into the sea and perish

or

reluctantly to go on
among the living"
[Od. 10.49-52]

"My god,
     those men
     must have been
     giants, come
     on fast
     by the thousands,
     how they break
     the earth,
     how they
     snap from
     the very peaks
     such boulders—
     the mountaintops
     falling upon
     us like
     twilight, like
     dark.
My god,
     all my
     fallen comrades,
     all my
     dear friends,
     swollen with
     grey sea-foam and
     sunk from
     the wine-bright
     surface of
     the world,
     sunk below,
     sinking into
     noumenal depths
     where light
     never reaches.

My god,
    the world
    sinks in
    turns, in
    tides, in
    sea-surge
    predictability,
    into nothing.
    Into nothing.
Into the dark sand bottoms
of nothing."

"Bright smoke signals at a distance
mix with shining air just above
the cliffs dappled with spruce.
A dense wood stands between;
the venture now is from the edge,
from the seam of sea, earth, and sky
into the center.

Until that moment
I had only dared the periphery,
the broad outer way that keeps cycling
through fit-and-start beginnings.

But that smoke—somewhere a flame
steadily flashes, merging itself with
the sun-glare of aether, starting the sky
to burn. That flame may be divine,
the divine center of things.

So I seek, striving to find the world-hearth
out of which all smoke-imaged things arise."

"Towards the center as a way in: fission.
The divine always splits."

"A hermeneutical presence,
        like a cloud-to-ground lightning flash
        in midday,
        instantaneous,
rends the veil of nature,
presses the wisdom
of the ages into my palm:

        what rises, what falls, what remains.

I will never tell.

The hollow stalk, withering
even as it is delivered,
the shimmering seed within it—

        be steady, stay yourself even as you
        cross sacred boundaries where
        identity is revealed
        as a metamorphic stream
        coursing through bodies,
        a particle shower of elements.

Remember the smoke, its fire,
the hearth where it burns.
Focus yourself into yourself:
        the hermeneutic passage is transformation.
Knowing this is your talisman,
a pharmakon pressed out of the
eternally rising fall of being."

"Such longing for unity overcomes
a man who feels his whole life
has been but a series of rifts, always
and always coming undone. The veil
fell from me in the presence
of divinity, in the absorption
through which all time vanished—
            the veil fell from the goddess
            of veils, the goddess whose mind
            translates itself ever
            into the outwardness of those mortals
            whom she encounters.
            She translates all
            who pass into her realm.
            The veil fell from this goddess,
            fell from this goddess along
            her divine back-curve already
            bare and beginning to disappear,
            around those ankles
            rotating in their eternal
            state, and fell between us,
            she, guiding me in the secrets
            of ecstasy, ecstasy, the divine
            loss, the subtle, releasing,
            the palpable of desire, the palpable
            drown in the sweetness
            of everything ethereal,
            in the sweetness of everything.
In the divine you cease, you cease and desire
is translated with an ineffable precision—which is
to say, with complete loss—into what thought
and words can never reach."

"The hearth
is only the entry:
you must seek the dead.

To pass
towards
the center,
submerge
into the final black
of oblivion,

become a shadow
in the depth of night.

This is the only way."

Who could frame with his eyes the divine,
its back and forth churn,
when the god does not wish to be seen?
[Od. 10.573-574]

ODYSSEY XI

MYTHOLOGY III

"Cut through the darkness,

cut the sail-slack and hoist in
        the wind sent by the god,

cut the sand and glistening sea-foam
        and the dark coast just ahead,

cut a path through sea-shine always
        trained west to dark sea-mists

cut heels into the land of Night
        drawing from the smooth sea
        a ship black in the total blackness

cut black earth where the lordly Sun's
        panoptic shine & gaze
        never, never glows

cut the earth into right angles measured
        by the long strength of my
        living arm

cut within the sacred square the dreadful
        silence, the impossibly quiet
        throats of sleek sacrificial beasts,
        their pulsing blood saturating
        the surrounding black empty,
        black blood mixing with Night
        and returning itself to the realm
        of the Unseen—"

"—let honey mix on the dark soil
    with milk and water and wine

gave the dark mouths of the dead some
    drainage out of the still-flowing
    vitality of liquid surfaces

spoke many incantations to the dead
    and to the mighty god of Absence,
    the unspeakable terror of Silence,

total Silence, the goddess reigning
    unwillingly over all living things,
    and to the dread goddess Night,

to her cloak of limitless blackness
    and her veil, which men call death,
    that is already covering those

whose strong arms still carve
    the world into a site
    of the not-yet—

and then the dread, the dread, the horror
    arose inside me
    and I was breathing it

and it was a mist all about me,
    it was my own blood,
    it was the sap

of every shoot and stalk, the essence
    of life that trembled
    in the face of such

utter emptiness and dark."

"By our living-light
we give to the dead
their appearance

while the dead in
their vanishment
illuminate our ways,

for they dwell
in the darkness
beneath all action

where in the long silence
out of all reckoning
beginnings & ends

converge, turning
in the unseen
loam of earth's

continual possibility"

You strive for a return sweet and fluid,
shimmering man of pain,
but god will make things tough and bitter
[*Od.* 11.100-101]

"In the deeps of the world beyond any light,
in the deeps where dark breaths blow
in the darkness and sweep across the broad
valley of emptiness, there I brought
blood, shining blood even as it flowed
black in the gaping blackness, and the
voice of the dead was wrested out
of silence by what little gleam
trickled in the holy blood-streams.

And the dead spoke and knew me
and knew the gods and their high designs
and all suffering and all possibility
were laid out before the mind
that makes itself but a shadow,
less, less than a shade
within dark's insurmountable gravity,
a dark shadow upon the midnight
of eternal midnight, torch-wipes
on the essence of extinguishment.

And the dead spoke a haze of words
that has become the atmosphere of my life,
unforgettable, urgent, complete:

     'Either way, suffering grips you,
     guides you, endures *as* you.
     You *are* suffering.
     Reach out into this
     swiftly passing world,
     know the sea,
     seek and find those
     who do not know it,pity them, show them
     signs of life lived

as the sea; *be the sea.*
Stretch out into
the solid earth, leaving
yourself behind
for a time, glittering on its shores,
then gather yourself
back into yourself,
be a mirror of the lunar
spin, the human spin
from bright fullness
to scarce outlines
all on a black background
of a dark beyond.'"

"the soul flees just like a dream"
[*Od.* 11.221]

out
of the silent
wells into which
speaking falls

the echoing
magic of speech
held them

thundering
down the halls
full of shadow
[*Od.*11.333-334]

"this night
so vast,
unspeakably
vast

there is time
for sleep
when it comes

for now
tell me
more

unfold
for me
those marvels
which only you
have seen"
[Od.11.373-374]

"They just keep coming,
this register of souls,
this calendar of souls,
asthmatic, pale,
images of men who shook
the ground as they fell and fell
into dark."

ODYSSEY XII

MYTHOLOGY IV

"How many deaths do we die
with every sun tipping over
the western limit while night closes in,
ever-ending, ever-enjambing
and driving loss into the center of everything—

with every tomb built or mound
piled to give the dead to the earth
their smoke already taken by the sky
with every grain from stalks fallen
under the scythe—

—look now,
so many deaths
around us,
in us

          we pass each moment
          within it, breathing it, filling
          ourselves with what has gone—

every appearance is a disappearance.

How many deaths do we die?

Back and forth across the island's seam
a whole ship full of men with each step
sinking beneath them, a ship of men
gathered fallen wood, severed limbs
from trunks, standing where the shore
reaches to heaven inside island trees,
carrying them across the dark sand and
stacking hewn wood to burn the fallen,
bones finding the downward path returning
to earth, flesh, hair, and blood the upward path
to sky, and our feet in the shifting sand, sinking."

"All your drive, roving and making the sea barren
and the earth scorched with your yearning, all that reaching
after what is ahead, the westward-falling future you want to claim:

> remember the dead, remember that there is
> a place where all horizons collapse,
> a field of presence like blackest night.

Remember this, let the past show you what is ahead.

Remember this as you slide over the bright sea and as the sun
resonates in everything under his gaze—waves, wake, shore,
sea-birds and their luminous feathers, sand and rock
and big cattle with long horns glaring the light like beacons.

Remember this: you cannot catch the light."

> "if you cause suffering
> the divine signs are clear:
>
> ruin for your ship
> and
> your crew
>
> and for you, if you survive:
>
> a return alone
> strung through many years
> and full of evils"
> [Od. 12.139-141]

"One voice summons all life,
moving like light across the surface
of the water, shadowing the foam-touched
sea that shines beneath.

Nothing escapes this sound like light:
pierces phenomena, threads every
breath and rustle into itself, any stirring
it alone carries and sustains.

So the voice streamed singular out
of the world's mouths, one voice binding
all minds and purposes to itself:

> *Come,*
> *come,*
> *your own suffering*
> *beckons you,*
> *your own grief*
> *will speak and enter*
> *the current*
> *of song*
> *a single voice sings.*
>
> *Come,*
> *come,*
> *your own suffering*
> *is a slack sail*
> *and only the voice*
> *will lift and fill it.*
>
> *Come,*
> *come,*
> *all flow into the one voice.*
> *Only what is unified is whole.*

That world-song, like all the seasons of the year
at once, like the sun and moon and stars pressed
into a single irresistible fire, or wave,
a wave of light that burns and consumes

and leaves nothing behind."

"all at once
signs and tokens
flashed before us
from the divine"
[*Od.* 12. 394]

"How could anyone hide from the sun

his saffron-light
clothing and kindling
all that moves

flaming
the inner fire
of animation?"

"only once
do things rise
with such
clarity into
mythology"
[*Od.* 12.452-453]

ODYSSEY XIII

HYPNOSIS

speaking came to rest
and heavy silence
enfolded them
through the wide hall
filled with shadows
and they were held
by the wonder of speech
[Od. 13.1-2]

Yearn for evening
draw down the sun's beams
with desire for home

All human suffering sets
and a night of grave force
settles over things

Across the whole arc of adversity
that constitutes a human life
pull at the light turn your face
again and again
towards the sun

Watch it sinking into dark night

this journey, a funeral—

on a dark and wide open sea
a black vessel packed with loaves
and wine the color of faded and fallen
roses or of the first dawn-slash
in the deep sky or of the final
blood-red embers aglow
on the world's circumference—
the wine, the bread, the bright gifts
that flash in the fading light,
a curiously wrought chest
to store what props us
for our momentary balance
in this endlessly falling life—
everything in order,
everything in its time

this is the appointed journey
to that island of beginning,
a cycle curling at last
back into itself

upon a grave brow sweet sleep fell,
irresistible, sweet, so close, so very close,
just like death
[Od. 13.79-80]

sleep now, sleep and forget
for a while what you have endured
that suffering both before you and behind

sleep and let the past and future
surge and crest and sink again
into the fathomless sea of the mind

sleep now and lapse into that oblivion
out of which memory and action awake

So great a choice to return, so heavy, so vast
to re-enter mortality, sail with swift winds
and long oar-strokes back into the harbor of becoming,
its high promontories encircling the sea-churn.

Once you dreamed of a cave filled with household things,
stone jugs, looms, amphorae all belonging to goddesses
in wine-dark shawls and eternally young,
glistening like mist settled on sun-touched shoulders.

Where is that cavern? What mortal could enter
the deepest places, discover the twin-gate in the dim
            recesses of the world?

You have left that path in your decision to return
and the ways are shut to you once more. Even in dreams
you can no longer see them; the earth is too dark,
the water too much like air clouded with fog.

The memory slips as you reach for it.

Two gates yawn in the dream-light
and in an instant reveal the great divide
as the cave-dark verges on snapping shut again:

One is ever down-going, ceaselessly falling,
imperiously towing under all living things
and wavering in eerie sea-green and wine-dark light,
an underground aurora borealis of vanishing.

Whither the other none can say—
all speaking belongs to the fall, only pretending to rise.
This second path recoils at any advance
of your dreaming mind or pitched song
or rush of thought. The second is a double path:
the path of the dead and of what shimmers
          beyond the veil.

          Gods cover the earth
          veiling what is,
          veiling mind
          from itself.

          Everything known
          in all regions
          of time and earth,
          everything
          that once passed
          through thought and word,
          memory itself is lost
          under such dense cover
          sent from above.

Earth and air, water and fire
bond and stray
like thought,
like words,
like all those
who wander
across the living earth
for a time.

All memory fades
and origins vanish
and the veil of divinity
waves in air and sunlight
and is gone.

What was known
becomes unknown
and the unknown
leaves traces, is a veil
contouring the shapes of what was.

And then: recollection.

speech will unveil
for you numberless
troubles at hand
in poetic halls
[Od. 13.306-7]

a many-headed frenzy
has crowded those cavernous halls
over the long rest of absence
a thousand voices echo
thunderous along emptiness
shatter the vacancy
once thought to be secure

you are become a name

vacuous, intoned, wingèd,
the noise of a shaped breath

the hour approaches to fill the word *full*
of sound and fury everything
signifying everything signifying
the manifold of being singular

ODYSSEY XIV

THE SELF AS OTHER

Long ago men were swine.
So common.
Just eat and drink and wallow in arousal.
Ordinary life.

Waking, finally, the mind cannot speak.
Mind remembers ocean, its patterned lunge and withdrawal.
So easy.
So easy to forget that second move,
so easy to be one who does not recede.
For now you are earth once more.

Past.
All that has now passed.
Long ago men were swine.
Now age has buckled you.
Steps of uncertainty sway beneath the weight of age.
So common.

In eyes once clear a haze recalls ocean's withdrawal.

Into the fenced yard, past swine and sows,
muck-filled stalls carefully planned,
kneeling before dogs scarcely this side of wild.

Out of the distance calls an old man, no longer swine.
Bend.
A man's voice belongs to thought and thought recedes.
No longer swine, man has withdrawn to the edge of the island of becoming.
Long ago abandoned.
Unwillingly.

Remember what you left behind. It has grown and changed without you. They are more than they were. And you? How could you measure change, enumerate gain and loss? An impossible economy of self. Didn't you give yourself to this long ago? You knew the gods and the gods knew you—but that was a knowledge drawn from the turning of empty into empty.

Such as yourself.

the gods themselves veiled
[*Od.* 14.357]

To speak about the self
is to schism one
that never really was
towards two
that collide and multiply
into the myriad of phased tones
that sing that speaking self.

To speak is to schism
and to sing the polyphonic
many-turning mystery.

nights under cold
millennial-aged starfire
bitter rain pellets
freeze in the drop
to earth reeds and sedge
stiff with freeze
knock and clack
on the north wind

borrow from yourself
what you forgot

nothing is simply given

another body emptied
that place where you lie
the wind emptied its cold pockets
where winter river-brush
could sound and sway

the night is full of empty

the empty is full of memory
of stars and their long-dead light

but nothing is so full
to stop the rain

ODYSSEY XV

SKYSIGNS

Outside the past, fate rolls, perpetual,
inside a present steered ever towards
what has not yet been. It belongs to
tomorrow, to that generation just now
waking into porticoes full of shadow,
and, most of all, to one among them
who never slept, eyes beaming
through the dark night, seeking a future
        more vivid.
Fate belongs to tomorrow but the gods
render it again and again inside the empty
        of now

        the past
        is the impression of fate
        left
        in the shifting sands
        of the present

                        the sun set and shadows covered every way
                        [*Od.* 15.185]

There was
in the open sky
after dawn
a parable given:

    eagle,
    winging over the plain
    leaving eyrie
    and mountains
    and their snow-crowned
    peaks glistening
    in the distance of morning,
    talons full of a goose or gander
    fattened over three years
    on the grain and meal
    gathered from swaths
    of dust-grey
    and burnished fields
    outlined and punctuated
    by silver olive groves—

from the queen's face,
almost divine, shadows
launching themselves
by the thousands
over her eyes' dark
and gleaming ocean
shadows pass
like souls expiring
from her fathomless mouth:

    "eagle is man
    soars through
    sea-like air
    hungering"

In an instant
the parable becomes
an omen

Wine-dark sky
crossed suddenly
by an eagle

libations pooling
in the hard
winter dust

the pool of wine
the air
shuddering

the stiff ground
trembling—
mind spasms

into what
has been known
and seen

twists
the distance
thence and hither

folding rigidly
bends into rigid
into necessity

time's canyon
spanned
an eagle

a directive
a god's gesture
into the next

Out of dark into dark
the plashing oars
dip and dip—

that wind, sent by a god, is gone.

the sun went down and every course fell into shadow
[*Od.* 15.296]

ODYSSEY XVI

REVELATIONS I

Dawn
out of the deep night
came swiftly,
rose-light, painted
by delicate fingers,
enthroning
all living creatures.
Men in the fields
sitting by embers
praise her distant heat.
Sailors
move swiftly
to harbor,
oars glistening
in the light
given by the sea
given by the sun—
they lower the sails,
let fall the anchor.
Disembarking
they send prayers
in wine to those below
and on the pluming smoke
into the morning air
to the gods who hold
heaven.
At once,
out of the dawn-
streaked sky
a hawk shoots
through the bright air,

messenger of death,
quick as light.
Everything points
to something else.
Watch.

Listen.

Inside what was once yours
you huddle. This is still
the rim of your history,
inside but peripheral.
The more you hide
the more you remember,
the more you dissemble,
the more you become
yourself. The past
is now before you,
drawing you into
what has been determined
from the beginning.

the light of the gods does not fall on everyone
[Od. 16.161]

this anaphora of concealment
and revelation is the gods' gift

repeat yourself through the syntax
of being, declining, polyptotonic,

turning and twisting in your fall

Generation gathers you back
to the center no span of time
no volume of experience—
no matter how vast—could refute.

What poured from you
as the body of desire momentarily stilled,
that mystery, *tenebrous & profound*, of creation,
still sways what remains within you.

This is the deepest impression,
that which can be represented,
the will stirring every appearance,
the form molding all instantiation.

Generation shows you the interior
that suffering, fear, & roaming
the dark foam-cresting sea
enfold in the cloak of impermanence.

Unfurling, moving paradox
from the inside, creation lifts the veil.

Those fanning arms
of a son, his joy
in beautiful auras
all around him
sweeping towards you.

Come to rest in that instant.

That embrace.

The way your breaths
fit each other.

Nothing, not even a god,
could cleave the momentary
single contour
of yourselves.

That father you were that
son you were that
husband you were
that revolution
you were
that wave
you were

collapsing and collapsing
in embrace a son you
only ever thought
now standing
eye-to-eye
eyes

swimming with those
questions you
remember those
unanswerables
that always
require
pursuit

and eyes filling with
vision of you vision
of you vision of
you you needing
the son you
needing to
be the
father
look

closer look closer standing
before you the ultimate
doctrine of the holy
ones know your-
self know
yourself
know

yourself

Woman moves across the floor
into the column of luminous air
near the central hearth.

Men crowd the hall, lean over
bright wine and meat
that do not belong to them.

There is a house faraway
where this is taking place.

Like gods, the men contrive
another's end.

Like Fate, she declares, half in shadow,
herself, like Fate, herself
and the negative of negation.

Uncertainty, evasion, desire
imbue waking life. The region
of force also contains quiet,
weakness, failure. So to sleep
and the dream of emancipation—

their minds turned towards rest
and they reached out for the greatest gift:
sleep.
[Od. 16.481]

ODYSSEY XVII

THRESHOLD

Song keeps beginning, dawning,
glinting early light into the buoyant air
into the fields laced with vetch
barley and frost, pathways
for the glare of beginning.

Song opens the world into itself,
into blossoming light that casts
luminous petals over byways
and the vistas they thread.

Song rings in the dawn-fissure,
inside the distance, along the many
curved paths of the world.

Song turns in the earliness of dawn
towards home and what was lost.

Song echoes in the light.

Song echoes in the light.

Song begins the dawning world,
waking the seam of here and gone.

Song frays the seam, showering
through-shine into the gap,
edging down now glimmering trails.

Song within openness returns
long-scattered petals of light
back into the center, still uncoiled
threads along the horizon of thought.

Song keeps beginning, dawning,
glinting early light upon bronze-
tipped spear points on hafts of ash,
upon cold, polished thresholds
mirroring the glare of beginning.

Shuttle dazzles and wefts across the loom,
whirls in the between. When did life shuttle
you into latitude, moving in the between?

The feeling of loss, long ago established,
is lost in the fabric hanging on the loom
where nothing is lost. Over, under, across,
and through—the cloth does not forget.

The loom's trabeation, archetype of temples,
squares and binds and bounds the artifice
your mind has built to dwell, weaving,
wafting and rising, until ligatures, unraveling,
                    snap

> the two came to a standstill
> as the hollow lyre
> poured its voice
> in rings around them
> [Od. 17.261-2]

Everything has awaited your return
across ocean's undulating back,
storm-beset and grey as winter,
through dull-hulled days, bleak,
under the gravity of night's shadows,
from stone-encircled cities to islands
azure and verdant in the center
of the divine sea, nacreous and deep,
amid thought human and divine,
archaic, built from field stone,
the bones of earth stolen
prior to the sky and its heaven
to which they now point.

Under an almost empty moon
the old dog on a rubbish heap,
his speed burned into frailty,
lifts his ashen face to catch the wind
that bears the master's voice.
Wind lifts a sigh into itself
as death sinks out of the evening.

a heaven wrought of iron
[*Od.* 17.565]

That woman from
across the wide hall
weaves all the light
and air filling
the distance
between you.

She is not waiting.
Did you forget
how many veils
she has cut
from her loom,
how she, too,

yearns and casts
and recasts
and ties knots
with words,
tangling surfaces
with surfaces?

All those years
have turned her
beyond what memory
might have contained
before, in the distance,
once, when the light

played on surfaces
with joints and
edges, surfaces
of textures of light
caught in them.
Light that fell on the hinges,

on the seams, where the
one was built, the other
woven, and the world
of contact generated
energies, threads, horizons.

twilight, already coming on
[*Od.* 17.606]

ODYSSEY XVIII

OVERTURES

Blood across the twilight
seeping into the brittle air
and into the breath
of stooping figures
within the court's breadth.
Toughened sandals
grit the fricative sand
on a limestone threshold
and whitewashed plaster floor.

Only a hint of violence, at first
in the air, in the sagging light.

Beginning is violence, a rending
of what was, to that very instant
of beginning, a unity of silences,
all at once shattered as if struck.

The force of origination
finally gathered at the descent of night,
for now a waxing shadow in the dark.

     Growling belly that is man
     beats the body, grounds the heel
     into turf into thud.

     Belly-grumble stoops the upright face,
     bends the eye to itself to prey
     and turns what is seen to prey.

     Rumble as if thunder in your head
     were the whole sky trembling,
     as if the gods quake the thronging vault

of mind and in-dwell to the sound
of one hand clapping and the snap
of teeth and jaw echoing in the skull.

Thrumming belly at the waist
drums the hollow to beat a war-drum,
heavy, empty, sounding thunder into the air beyond

to which the eyes are drawn.

of all things
breathing and creeping
along the ground
the earth brings forth nothing
more wretched than man
[Od. 18.130-131]

Encircling mind entangles.

Her cheeks and lips and wide eyes
shine brightly in the glow
the goddess has bestowed on her,
coiling through the smoke-filled chambers
as she leans against the thick hearth-column
bathed in light.

She leans against the column,
a statue of herself, taller, firmer,
radiant in the divine grace—
the statue crafted over many years, carved
by sorrow & loss, by desire, by all the gifts of god.

Her own mind wove the cloth draping her now,
covering the image of herself.

The woman, left long ago,
hangs loops of thought and speech on the loom
of dissemblance, central to the court.
And the words rise in circles, entangling minds:

If you thought I was beautiful
this hall would be filled
with gleaming gifts.
But I am not;
the gods destroyed all the loveliness
of my youth in the hour of his departure.

So the inscrutable tangles, simple and concise,
widen in circles of tense retribution
while the hall fills with gifts.

Delight resonates from the wondrous gifts
as they are brought before the lady
and her encircling mind:
  a richly embroidered gown
  intricately lovely, a dozen golden clasps
  gleaming upon it;
  a necklace strung with gold
  and amber beads, a masterwork
  radiant as dark sun-fire;
  earrings in clusters of three beads
  like sweet, dark mulberries
  sparkling with dewy elegance.
If only destiny were swayed by the lavish gestures
and the curious gleam of such gifts.

Dance and song that flames the soul
shook all into delicate frenzy
where they remained
as evening came on.

Soon their revelry was covered
in the settling black dusk of night.
[Od. 18.304-5]

ODYSSEY XIX

REVELATIONS II

Into the underground vault
two shadows are cast
lengthening miraculously
by the torch of divinity
that follows them,
an invisible flame
composed by the god
who writes white fire
across the night's depth.

Gather and preserve
what once seemed tokens,
for they are signifiers
of a history of self,
a household once blessed
and trembling now
in the verge of blessedness.

Each item to be stored
bears another's sweet light glinting
into the gravity of midnight,
discrete moons whose gleam
always guides thought
as from air into water
into the refraction of phenomenality.

Fashion an object of yourself.

Place it before the object of your desire.

Praise them both, becoming like a god,
author of a poetry of selfhood.

Laying out deception
upon deception
one speaks along the seam
of what is veiled
and what is bare
[*Od.* 19.203]

Indeed, the very fact of his disguise,
when seen as such, implicated him
to be other than himself, and so clearly
shown to be none other than himself.

Her gaze unmasks him, deepened by years of longing,
two decades of the difficult, luminous desire
of imagination, decades instructing her
in the tender erotics of hope, loss, and suffering.

Once the two walked together slowly
down to the sacred cave of the island's nymphs
and the Muses, far to the west of the city limits,
along the narrow, foam-kissed strand they went,

each of them learning the secrets of intimacy,
as the cave's darkness swallowed them entire.

In the high oaks
the voice of god
clamors, a wind
through still bare
and dark limbs.

Hear it
as your breath
suspends itself
between intake
and exhale.

The god speaks
in the trees,
in the air
and the force
of wind.

The god speaks.

Of the light of day
and heaven's
eternal night.

Of human passion
in its fullness
where suffering
and ecstasy
merge.

Of frailty,
human life,
thinning tips
of the great tree of being
reaching into
the remote, dark sky.

One more night
reeling the world
under its turning
and beneath
the vanished moon
the past and future
will collide.

sitting on the edge, turned at once towards the shadows
[Od. 19.389]

Following the moon's orbit
and its aureola, faint, ethereal,
backlighting sparse cloud cover,
a boy journeys across the water
to become a man.

Many cycles have passed since that instant under sun-glare,
catching fire to the bronze spear point
and thrusting long shadows along the steep ground
from the heavy shaft of ash, the instant of skirmish
as lowered shoulders thrash the brush,
tusk on fire like the spear point of bronze opposing it,
a shadow quick as light casting itself against the boy,
manhood closing in, blood bright in the sun-filled air,
tusk and bone glistening, bronze losing itself
in thick bristled hide that falls upon the mountain's shoulders.
Incantations and dressings start to close the rent flesh
cycled to scar white as tusk and bone,
touched with silver as moonlight

now threatening a rupture
once more. Where you were split
and healed remains a trace
impossible to disguise,
the name given you
by the body's cycle
through the world of light.

Double are the gates through which
        dreams pass

there, in the mind, in the soul,
        where everything is doubled.

Dreams move on the horizon
        of thought,

on the dividing rim where polarities
        touch,

inner and outer, self and other,
        mortal and immortal.

In the dream the two gates
        are of hewn ivory

and polished horn, and as the dream
        is spoken,

the division of ivory and horn,
        of fading away

and coming to light, recedes into
    an aetheric

possibility, heavy with mist, distant
    as a horizon,

touched to glisten here and there
    by an inscrutable light.

ODYSSEY XX

ALLEGIANCES & SILENCE

All is quiet
in the house
where one does not sleep.

Where the goddess
bestows
what she will.

The house is quiet.

A voice
in the darkness
shatters the mind,

that shimmering,
dissembling,
calculating mind

shattered in the quiet house.

The goddess
demands
negation.

All those shimmering pieces

strewn across
the polished floor's
smoothness.

Still sparkling,
reflecting always
the light

bestowed by the goddess of night.

Think how close they are,
those whom you love, lying
behind walls as thick
as you built them
in the beginning.

Into the ornamented forecourt now laden with the light of morning
cattle, goats, sheep, and swine are led by men whose memories
        will soon be put to the test.

The marketplace has emptied itself for the day's festival
honoring the god of annihilation, the Dread Light God of the Future.
        There was no moon last night

and the sunset burned red as blood across the western shore
of an early spring night, cold and deep as the ocean
        whose rolling waves surround the world.

At a distance, the women of morning work their grain
into flour at the stone set in place by the island's lord
        dispersed like a mist long ago,

pausing for an instant to mark the sky,
the eastern edge of the world as clear as glass and rippled
        by the rattling thunder of the great god.

They know, all of them, with a certainty as clear as the sky
as clear as glass and rippled by the god's heavy thunder,
        the fate reverberating through this sign,

piercing heaven and earth at once, the grand tumult of destiny
shaking the ocean-wrapped world. They know, all of them,
        the unseen lightning to follow.

And what it means.

        Maybe there were women rushing
        in ecstasy to shake the great tree
        and summon the imperious god
        into presence. Maybe all the townspeople
        processed solemnly through the broad
        and vacant town square up
        to the cave sanctuary bearing numerous
        resplendent gifts for the god hidden
        somewhere overhead. Maybe
        several picked boys and girls
        with long hair streaming or braided
        sang a hymn, a paean, and danced
        in a ring before the palace's
        exotic horns of consecration.
        Maybe the expectation of the god's presence
        induced a certain mentality, a receptivity
        in the group's collective mind. Yet
        the tree stirs in the wind, shaking, shaken,
        the cave echoes whatever sounds

in its shadowy mouth, the horns of beasts
grow long and curl into sky, the mind opens
in its gesture of uplift as if they—minds,
horns, cave, and tree—are pointing
to whatever pulls them ceaselessly upward.

Against the backdrop of reverence
where the festivity unfolds
some cast long shadows of hubris
darkening that future always
behind their backs and beyond
          their view.

Shameless, irreverent, blind
to the growing threat among them,
the native antagonism between
one and many and the improper
regard for the surging power
          of the singular.

*"so much better to die
than to witness such atrocities"*
[Od. 20.316-317]

ODYSSEY XXI

TENSION, URGENCY, EMERGENCE

All thought now
comes from the goddess,
the soul ignited
by her firelight eyes—
two birds, flaming, bronze,
calling the iron song
of thought
into the wakeful mind,
stirring the soul's bird
and its own birdsong
that calls in response
and rises and, aloft,
now sings the song
of the gods.

Every object casts shadows and rich luster
over the eyes, the mind. They exist
more in memory than anywhere else.
Where the shadow's depths and ruddy
burnt light quiver like cymbals
wider and lower through the mind's vault
vibrating all that is stored within.

What is kept hidden will remain so
until the dark earth, too dense to resonate,
will gather everything back to itself—
memory and the bone chamber housing it,
the bow and its long quiver and the arrows
whose shadows elongate in flight,
groaning men falling beneath them
and the high-roofed chambers
of the house where you sit.

in that moment
sunlight was fading
over their grief
[Od. 21.226]

Striving to bend
one end to another,
as a lyre or a bow,
the many burn themselves
into exhaustion.

They are now but a heap of ashes.
Precisely what you needed.

Shuffle the others out of the light,
sequestering them into some high chamber
or else in the deepest recess of the great house.

Evacuate the mind of what debris
clutters a view of what is before you.

Past & future slip and recede
into the tense between, the one that is
stretched across, binding ends together,
pulling distance into phenomenal collapse,
sweeping through the vanishing of itself.

Urgency flickers to life
out of the immensity
of endurance.

Presence, finally, opens itself
as the impossible volume of light
held by the bronze tip
of an arrow.

Nothing, not even the years
of waiting, of narrowing hope,
of dread infusing loss

nothing has been inchoate
in this life.

Presence, at last, rises
and raises all thought
and action
into its ever-expansive light.

Out from under beauty
arose a song
like a calling bird
[*Od.* 21.411]

A single arrow rushes through a narrow field
made by axes leaned against the porch's columns.

Silence, wonder, and outrage grip those who watched
a swiftening shadow thud and elapse into the darkness
of the long hall.

A head nodding, blazing feet, arms flash
out of now empty sheaths. Bronze flickers again
and again inside this instant, this fathomless,
irreconcilable instant out of nowhere.

ODYSSEY XXII

REVELATIONS III

Unclothed mind twists continually, slips
from the cover of dissemblance
now cast upon the turning floor of necessity.

Surging mind lunges the body into position
upon the wide stone threshold, *grasping the bow
and quiver full of shafts, pouring out arrow after
fleet arrow on the floor before his feet.*

Speech twists into the tightly knit air
between presences and presencing:

"May the grim God of Distances
grant that I hit the mark
now within my sights, one
hitherto untouched."

The cup rimmed with gold, being raised
to a silent, grinning mouth, held wine
of sea-deep hue that lapped the edge
as if straining now to spill, to drop
and disperse across the level floor
where all directions are open.

Unclothed mind of continual torque
turns itself towards that which is always
contrary and twists it from itself.

*Who would ever believe that,
among a vast plurality of living, feasting men,
the singular, though full of so much force,
could bring all-consuming death
and sable woe?*
[Od. 22.12-14]

Arrows pouring from the threshold
thicken the air filled with dust
kicked up by men falling
face first into the expectant earth.

Din begins, guttural, anxious,
out of the stun at fury unveiled at last.

Blood spurts from throats and innards
laid bare to the relentless light
shed over the whole place
by the Apollonian and illustrious sun
finishing the world's bronze surface
with its dense and voluminous glare.

The whole bronze world clashes ceaselessly
as if the substance of things
is groping constantly for the return
of bronze to bronze.

towards an innerness full of light,
full of light
[*Od.* 22.121]

After arrow-clatter settles,
long shadows range
over the floor
from heavy spears,
tips aflame with bronze.

A voice skates over the surface
of the blood and slows
as it meets the postured resistance
of a man like a falcon, telescopic
eyes, nobility emanating
from the grace by which he dives
again and again against his prey
already taken in the crimp
of fear, death flashing continually
on the faces, eyes, and minds,
resonating in the tremor within
as if from without

and the voice is pleading
in rings of quiver from the throat,
terror propelling it into the falcon's view
where it is turned to prey.

            all that death
            upon death—piling bodies
            seeping the once-animating life
            from hewn limbs,
            breasts, necks and heads
                    asunder—

                    all that death
                somehow determined
            by deeply riven gods
            of marble sinew
            and mystery
            somehow required, as if
            to make way for the restoration
            of a holy unity

it is unholy to boast
over the fallen
[Od. 22.412]

Gore-spattered hall falls silent
bereft at last of the loud, discordant
groaning.

A sere is now visible, as if
all the violence really had been
necessary.

Now, just as the moon begins to wither
just past full, so the finished cycle is
instantly

eclipsed by a dawning way, and the death-
howl, vanished, leaves room for the long-desired
dirge

purging the many living souls
gathered in the hall, now scrubbed
clean

and smudged with sulfur,
of grief and loss so suddenly
stripped

away from their pulsing,
empty, faith-ridden hearts, ready finally
to be full.

ODYSSEY XXIII

EUTHANASIA
OR, THE BOOK OF LOSS

Gray age hobbles towards a sleeping mind
full of dreams full of forgetting.

Enter the sleeping mind, the dreaming mind.
Dream the image of a self without desire.
A self of pure fulfillment.

Where could all that loss have gone?
All that incommensurable yearning
on yearning in the long night of memory—
let it slip away in the fullness
of the dream.

Awaken to denial, disbelief,

and most of all

to the fear of truth.

the spirit, always uncertain
[Od. 23.72]

Silent

as a tomb

you sit face-to-face.

The whole room
solemn as a grave.

Fulfillment now
would be a kind of death.

It is not easy to let go
of a longing so great.

the heart
always more relentless
than stone
[Od. 23.103]

"Everything we hid
for one
another
has become a sign—

remember
love comes first
and last—

what you had
to leave
for so long

and now
the final secret to be revealed."

Periphrastically
expectation
turned into my name.

How I knew
myself
through the nights
or, singular
as the remembrance
and sensation,
the long, dark night
where your absence
kindled this fire
that sustained me

which a return would
extinguish.

And then the cold.

"Still, tonight
        let the wedding dance
describe the orbit within our house
and love.

Yes, our love,
which has never needed
the cold reality of, say,
a singular deep night.

Our love is ever
in the plural
and always recoiling
between past and future."

the great house shook festively
beneath the footfalls of men dancing
and women in robes of deep folds
[Od. 23.146-147]

Carved into the trunk
of the ancient olive tree
that once marked a boundary
but now forms a post
leafed in gold, silver, and ivory
of an elaborate bed
at the center of a great house

can be discerned
faintly, in shallow
relief where the metal
has been pressed into it,
three lessons from desire:

because the mystery of generation
        is at the center of things

because the center of the mystery
        is the generation of things

because the generation of center
        is the mystery of things.

The entire house is built
to cover this confession.

        Follow the torchlight
        to the soft bed
        where you have not met
        since the days of youth
        now far behind you.

        Find the scars, the curves
        and valleys of bodies
        once familiar
        as your own skin.

Sink down into
the night's depth,
drawn out
towards the dawn
which the gods hold back

for discoveries
of selves and selves
and disclosures
of carefully chosen secrets.

When you wake

I will be gone.

Already the light of day
was upon the good earth
when the goddess of eyes
cloaked them in darkness
and led them out of the city
[Od. 23.371-372]

ODYSSEY XXIV

THEODICY

God of eternal down-going summons all
down into earth's midnight

where only his golden staff flashes,
mystifies,
awakens sleeping souls

into death

Cryptically speak events of life
to a vanquished soul
beneath the dark earth.

Seasons intimated the cycle
along which each life turns,
the swallows return to oak rafters
to fabricate nests of straw and twig
for the eggs that break
under the pressing upsurge of new life.

Memories dim in the earth's crowded
yet lonesome quiet, fold back
into the world-song unmarked
by personality.

And in each return to the all
what was hidden to souls
over-fixated on the monumental
traces the universal curves
of the open secret back
onto the vanquished

as clarity emerges in the dim
underground, echoing
in the dark crypt of the singular
as it is by night
unwoven.

just like the sun or the moon
[Od. 24.148]

The mind shimmers
beneath its dark
apparent stagnancy

waiting

charged by a desire
too deep to sound

waiting

apparently slumbering
while men busied themselves
with grasping,
contemptuously berated
the old man like a sleeping animal

until the sudden din of God's mind
awakens him.

In a world where everything hides
the prudent man seeks within things
what is covered.

The wise man, having discovered
in speech and mind, lets the covering remain.

Return to the source
alone.

Make your way
in dissemblance
through the orchard,
its familiar, gnarled limbs
and their spindled shadows
twisting darkly over furrows
carved by ancestors
long since ploughed
into the dust
of the fields they worked.
Their bones fill the air
and earth.

The source runs down with roots
seeking water of the underground.

Speak the source in your disguise,
let it pull you from the inside
back into itself
and then splinter you again.

clouds of woe black as night
gathered
and covered him
[Od. 24.315]

Bloodshed reduplicates
through the language of mastery.

The gods themselves are soaked
in constant overthrow
and struggle for dominion.

And behold! In their rise and fall
and rise and fall permeating the whole
how they glisten under the radiant sun!
How they flash like glare
over the earth's undulating waters!
How the spill and gush
slices the light into transfigured images
of eyes, bright eyes,
and the ever-shining
anterior mind!

silence
deep as a grave
gripping every last man
[Od. 24.441]

God the father,
greatest of all the world's powers,
put an end to my seeking:
what presence
does your thought
now conceal?
[Od. 24.473-474]

Bronze, mercilessly reflecting the light of midday,
envelopes force oppressing force.

The world in twain soon will shatter.

Out of heaven's clear upper air
god becomes man becomes bird.

All of nature attends these transformations,
understanding diffused throughout
as the mind of god.

Everywhere you turn
there is the turning.

From thunder-din to words to song,
so quickly flies the god's voice.

NOTES

This project emerged from a slow reading of the Greek *Odyssey* between spring, 2009 and spring, 2010. I used the third edition of Monro and Allen's two volume *Odysseae*, volumes III and IV in their *Homeri Opera* (Oxford: Clarendon, 1920). In *A Heaven Wrought of Iron*, the italicized text justified to the right sometimes translates, sometimes transfigures the Greek text indicated by the bracketed citation.

In several places I have woven lines, fragments, or language from other sources into the poems above. Some of these literary encounters— for I do not regard this as either "stealing" or "borrowing," but rather as collaboration & dialogue—are listed below as "notes." Due to the very nature of the project, there is an inherent relationship and in- or trans-fusion of imagery from the *Odyssey* throughout the text of *A Heaven Wrought of Iron*. For the vast majority of instances of this type of collaboration I have provided no references.

The *Odysseian* line δύσετό τ᾽ ἠέλιος σκιόωντό τε πᾶσαι ἀγυιαί, which appears frequently in the Greek, occurs also throughout the above text and is translated in various ways. I tried to account for every occurrence of this phrase in the Greek poem to give a reader of contemporary poetry in English a sense of this feature of Homeric poetry. It appears in the following places in *A Heaven Wrought of Iron*:

Book II, poem 4
Book III, poem 7
Book XI, poem 3
Book XV, poems 3 & 7

Book IV, poem 6: The fourth graph presents imagery found in the Delphic oracle's reply to Kroisos in Herodotos' *Histories* 1.47.

Book VI, poem 3: "lifted face": The reference is to Ovid, Book 1.84-6, *Metamorphoses* and the species-being, to use a Marxian phrase, that sets apart and distinguishes humanity:

> pronaque cum spectent animalia cetera terram,
> os homini sublime dedit caelumque videre
> iussit et erectos ad sidera tollere vultus.

Book IX, poem 1: The penultimate line echoes Melville's opening to *Moby Dick*.

Book X, poem 5: Language resonates with Tennyson's poem "Ulysses."

Book X, poem 10: Some of the language converses with Blake's "The Tyger."

Book XII, poem 4: This is a reading and a vision of the Sirens' Song.

Book XII, poem 6: Echoes language from Herakleitos, fragment 16, and from Martin Heidegger's essay "Aletheia: Heraklit, Fragment 16."

Book XIII, poem 6: Language is woven from threads of Lysander's speech at 1.1.141-149 of Shakespeare's *A Midsummer Night's Dream*.

Book XIII, poem 9: Italicized language in the second graph comes from Tennyson's "Ulysses" and in the fourth graph from Shakespeare's *Macbeth* 5.5.25-27.

Book XVI, poem 5: In the second graph Baudelaire's phrase "Dans une ténébreuse et profonde unité" from the poem "Correspondances" is the source of the phrase "tenebrous & profound." In the third graph echoes of Arthur Schopenhauer's *Die Welt als Wille und Vorstellung* can be heard.

Book XVI, poems 6 & 7: These particular poems are dedicated with the linked pair of joy & sorrow to my oldest child, Maya S. Spitzer: to the memory of your wonder-filled childhood, to the promise of your rising adulthood, to the moment of your widening adolescence.

Book XVI, poem 9: The language throughout this poem draws deeply from Jacques Derrida's essay, "Force and Signification."

Book XVII, poem 2: The imagery of the "loom's trabeation, archetype of temples," relies conceptually on Indra Kagis McEwen's *Socrates' Ancestor: An Essay on Architectural Beginnings* (Cambridge, MA: MIT Press, 1993).

Book XVIII, poem 4: The italicized language paraphrases and collapses Penelope's speech to the suitors at *Odyssey* 18.251-280.

Book XVIII, poem 5: The middle section describing the gifts translates *Odyssey* 18.292-298.

Book XIX, poem 1: The italicized language comes from my mother's 1950's *Webster's New Collegiate Dictionary* (the title page is missing), s.v. "refraction."

Book XIX, poem 5: Invokes Rilke's *Sonnette an Orpheus* 3, especially the final line: "Ein Hauch um nichts. Ein Wehn im Gott. Ein Wind."

Book XXII, poem 1: Lines 5-7 translate *Odyssey* 22.2-4; lines 10-13 translate part of Odysseus' speech at *Odyssey* 22.6-7.

Book XXIV, poem 11: The final two lines derive from *Odyssey* 24.164.

Books from Etruscan Press

Shadows of Houses | H. L. Hix

Wild and Whirling Words: A Poetic Conversation | Moderated by H. L. Hix

Art Into Life | Frederick R. Karl

Free Concert: New and Selected Poems | Milton Kessler

Who's Afraid of Helen of Troy: An Essay on Love | David Lazar

Parallel Lives | Michael Lind

The Burning House | Paul Lisicky

Quick Kills | Lynn Lurie

Synergos | Roberto Manzano

The Gambler's Nephew | Jack Matthews

The Subtle Bodies | James McCorkle

An Archaeology of Yearning | Bruce Mills

Arcadia Road: A Trilogy | Thorpe Moeckel

Venison | Thorpe Moeckel

So Late, So Soon | Carol Moldaw

The Widening | Carol Moldaw

Cannot Stay: Essays on Travel | Kevin Oderman

White Vespa | Kevin Oderman

The Dog Looks Happy Upside Down | Meg Pokrass

The Shyster's Daughter | Paula Priamos

Help Wanted: Female | Sara Pritchard

American Amnesiac | Diane Raptosh

Saint Joe's Passion | JD Schraffenberger

Lies Will Take You Somewhere | Sheila Schwartz

Fast Animal | Tim Seibles

American Fugue | Alexis Stamatis

The Casanova Chronicles | Myrna Stone

The White Horse: A Colombian Journey | Diane Thiel

The Arsonist's Song Has Nothing to Do With Fire | Allison Titus

The Fugitive Self | John Wheatcroft

YOU. | Joseph P. Wood

Etruscan Press is Proud of Support Received from

Wilkes University

Youngstown State University

The Ohio Arts Council

The Stephen & Jeryl Oristaglio Foundation

The Nathalie & James Andrews Foundation

The National Endowment for the Arts

The Ruth H. Beecher Foundation

The Bates-Manzano Fund

The New Mexico Community Foundation

Drs. Barbara Brothers & Gratia Murphy Fund

The Rayen Foundation

The Pella Corporation

Founded in 2001 with a generous grant from the Oristaglio
Foundation, Etruscan Press is a nonprofit cooperative of poets and
writers working to produce and promote books that nurture the
dialogue among genres, achieve a distinctive voice, and reshape the
literary and cultural histories of which we are a part.

etruscan press
www.etruscanpress.org

Etruscan Press books may be ordered from

Consortium Book Sales and Distribution
800.283.3572
www.cbsd.com

Small Press Distribution
800.869.7553
www.spdbooks.org

Etruscan Press is a 501(c)(3) nonprofit organization.
Contributions to Etruscan Press are tax deductible
as allowed under applicable law.
For more information, a prospectus,
or to order one of our titles,
contact us at books@etruscanpress.org.